A Note From Rick Renner

I am on a personal quest to see a "revival of the Bible" so people can establish their lives on a firm foundation that will stand strong and endure the test as end-time storm winds begin to intensify.

In order to experience a revival of the Bible in your personal life, it is important to take time each day to read, receive, and apply its truths to your life. James tells us that if we will continue in the perfect law of liberty — refusing to be forgetful hearers, but determined to be doers — we will be blessed in our ways. As you watch or listen to the programs in this series and work through this corresponding study guide, I trust you will search the Scriptures and allow the Holy Spirit to help you hear something new from God's Word that applies specifically to your life. I encourage you to be a doer of the Word He reveals to you. Whatever the cost, I assure you — it will be worth it.

> Thy words were found, and I did eat them;
> and thy word was unto me the joy and rejoicing of mine heart:
> for I am called by thy name, O Lord God of hosts.
> — Jeremiah 15:16

Your brother and friend in Jesus Christ,

Rick Renner

The Healing Ministry of Jesus

Copyright © 2021 by Rick Renner
P.O. Box 702040
Tulsa, OK 74170

Published by Rick Renner Ministries
www.renner.org

ISBN 13: 978-1-68031-986-6

eBook ISBN 13: 978-1-68031-987-3

How To Use This Study Guide

This four-lesson study guide corresponds to *"The Healing Ministry of Jesus" With Rick Renner* (Renner TV). Each lesson in this study guide covers a topic that is addressed during the program series, with questions and references supplied to draw you deeper into your own private study of the Scriptures on this subject.

To derive the most benefit from this study guide, consider the following:

First, watch or listen to the program prior to working through the corresponding lesson in this guide. (Programs can also be viewed at **renner.org** by clicking on the Media/Archives links.)

Second, take the time to look up the scriptures included in each lesson. Prayerfully consider their application to your own life.

Third, use a journal or notebook to make note of your answers to each lesson's Study Questions and Practical Application challenges.

Fourth, invest specific time in prayer and in the Word of God to consult with the Holy Spirit. Write down the scriptures or insights He reveals to you.

Finally, take action! Whatever the Lord tells you to do according to His Word, do it.

For added insights on this subject, it is recommended that you obtain Rick Renner's books *Sparkling Gems From the Greek, Volumes 1 and 2*. You may also select from Rick's other available resources by placing your order at **renner.org** or by calling **1-800-742-5593**.

TOPIC

The Types of Sicknesses Jesus Healed

SCRIPTURES

1. **Hebrews 13:8** — Jesus Christ the same yesterday, and to day, and for ever.

2. **John 21:25** — And there are also many other things which Jesus did, the which, if they should be written every one, I suppose that even the world itself could not contain the books that should be written. Amen.

3. **Matthew 4:23-25** — And Jesus went about all Galilee, teaching in their synagogues, and preaching the gospel of the kingdom, and healing all manner of sickness and all manner of disease among the people. And his fame went throughout all Syria: and they brought unto him all sick people that were taken with divers diseases and torments, and those which were possessed with devils, and those which were lunatick, and those that had the palsy; and he healed them. And there followed him great multitudes of people from Galilee, and from Decapolis, and from Jerusalem, and from Judaea, and from beyond Jordan.

4. **Mark 1:32-34** — And at even, when the sun did set, they brought unto him all that were diseased, and them that were possessed with devils. And all the city was gathered at the door. And he healed many that were sick of divers diseases, and cast out many devils; and suffered not the devils to speak, because they knew him.

5. **Mark 1:39** — And he preached in their synagogues throughout all Galilee, and cast out devils.

GREEK WORDS

1. "heal" — ἰάομαι (*iaomai*): to cure; to be doctored; a healing power that progressively reverses a condition; a progressive, restorative healing power; denotes healing that comes to pass over a period of time

2. "healing" — θεραπεύω (*therapeuo*): therapy; pictures a healing touch that requires corresponding actions; primarily used to describe the healing ministry of Jesus

3. "sickness" — νόσος (*nosos*): a terminal condition for which there is no known natural cure; in the ancient world, it especially described spirit-induced illnesses; this type of disease held no hope of recuperation; an unalterable, irreversible, incurable, permanent condition

4. "disease" — μαλακία (*malakian*): a crippling or debilitating form of sickness; weakness

5. "fame" — ἀκοή (*akoe*): an ear; denotes ears ringing or filled with information and news; hence, rumors or stories

6. "sickness" — ἀσθενεία (*astheneia*): an all-encompassing term for all types of sickness and disease; describes a person who is frail in health; one so physically weak that he is unable to travel; one who is feeble, fragile, faint, incapacitated, disabled, or simply in such poor health that it would be unthinkable to transport him; shut in or homebound; can also mean to be in financial need

7. "torments" — βάσανος (*basanos*): from the root word (*basano*); describes one that is tormented or one that is afflicted

8. "demonized" — δαιμονίζομαι (*daimonidzomai*): those that were demonized; under the influence of demons

9. "lunatick" — σεληνιάζομαι (*seleniadzomai*): moonstruck: an event that happened during the full moon; a sickness resulting from dabbling in the occult

10. "palsy" — παραλυτικός (*paralutikos*): those that were paralyzed; lame; bedfast

11. "brought" — φέρω (*phero*): to physically carry

12. "diseased" — ἔχω κακός (*echo kakos*): compound of *echo*, meaning to have something, and *kakos*, means something bad, really vile; compounded, *echo kakos* means miserably afflicted; extremely sick; in the last stage of their condition; a terminal case

13. "many" — πολλοὺς (*pollous*): the plural form of πολύς (*polus*), meaning a great number or multitudes

14. "cast out" — ἐκβάλλω (*ekballo*): compound word from *ek* meaning out, and *ballo*, means to throw; compounded, *ekballo* means to forcibly evict; to throw out; to cast out; to expel; to drive out; to kick out;

historically, it was used to describe a nation that forcibly deported lawbreakers from its borders

SYNOPSIS

The four lessons in this study on *The Healing Ministry of Jesus* will focus on the following topics:

- The types of sicknesses Jesus healed
- Exactly 'how' did Jesus heal the sick?
- The use of 'therapy' in Jesus' ministry
- Healing power for all who believe

The emphasis of this lesson:

There were different types of healing Jesus operated in when He ministered to the sick. There was no sickness, disease, or condition, no matter how difficult in the natural, that Jesus did not heal. He has not changed, and the same healing power is available to us today.

The Same Yesterday, Today, and Forever

The healing ministry of Jesus is demonstrated throughout the gospels. Jesus had a miraculous ministry while He walked on the earth, which is documented in the four gospels. Some may say, "Well, yes, that was then. But what about today?"

Hebrews 13:8 is a very foundational verse about the life and present-day ministry of Jesus Christ. It states, "Jesus Christ the same yesterday, and to day, and for ever." The phrase "the same" describes *something that is unchanging*. Who Jesus *was yesterday* is who He *is today* and is exactly who He *will be tomorrow*. What Jesus did yesterday is what He is doing presently and what He will be doing in the future. So if Jesus was the miracle-worker we read about in the gospels, He is still a miracle-worker today, and He will be a miracle-worker tomorrow.

The World Could Not Contain the Books

In concluding his letter, John said something interesting about the ministry of Jesus. In John 21:25 he recorded, "And there are also many other things which Jesus did, the which, if they should be written every one, I suppose that even the world itself could not contain the books that should be written. Amen." The phrase "I suppose" is from a Greek word which describes *an impossibility*. It could be translated "I suppose — of course, we know it is impossible. Jesus did more than could ever be recorded. But I suppose if it were feasible, if it were possible, even the world itself could not contain the books that should be written."

It is clear from this passage that we do not have a complete record of *all* the signs, wonders, healings, and miracles Jesus performed. In fact, there are a maximum of 53 events recorded about Jesus' ministry in the gospels and between 23 to 27 actual days of His life recorded. There isn't a single record of one full day in Jesus' life. However, we do have small snapshots — fragments of His healing ministry. Jesus' life was literally overflowing with the miraculous and with healing power.

It is important for us to understand the healing ministry of Jesus Christ. We need healing, our relatives and friends need healing, and others need healing — and it is still available today.

Iaomai Healing

In the Greek language, there are primarily two words to describe the healing ministry of Jesus — *iaomai* and *therapeuo*. The first word translated as "heal" is the Greek word *iaomai*, which means *to cure*. It denotes *healing that comes to pass over a period of time rather than instantaneous healing*. This translation, however, is not used often in the Scriptures — more often *iaomai* is translated as "doctor."

In Jesus' day, if people went to a medical doctor — an *iaomai* — they went to one who had the ability to progressively restore their health. When we seek the help of a physician today, do we expect an instantaneous, miraculous solution? Probably not. We would likely expect the doctor to prescribe something that would begin reversing our condition day-by-day, hour-by-hour, progressively bringing healing.

In addition to the multitudes who were instantly healed by Jesus, there were many other people who sought Him for healing who were not instantly cured. As Jesus released God's healing power by touching them or speaking over them, like medicine prescribed by a physician they received their healing progressively and over a period of time. We can find an example of one of these progressive healings in the gospel of Luke:

"And as he entered into a certain village, there met him ten men that were lepers, which stood afar off: And they lifted up their voices, and said Jesus, Master, have mercy on us. And when he saw them, he said unto them, Go shew yourselves unto the priests. And it came to pass, that, as they went, they were cleansed. And one of them, when he saw that he was *healed*, turned back, and with a loud voice glorified God, And fell down on his face at his feet, giving him thanks: and he was a Samaritan" (Luke 17:12-16).

The Word says, "...*As they went*, they were *cleansed*...." The healing power had been released into the lepers and healing immediately began working in their bodies. These ten lepers were *progressively* and *completely* made well. Look again at Luke 17:15: "And one of them, when he saw that he was healed..." In Greek, the word "healed" here is *iaomai*. From the moment they encountered God's healing power released through Jesus, a progressive, restorative work began to take place.

Therapeuo Healing

The second word used to describe healing in the gospels is the Greek word *therapeuo*. This word is probably used 95 percent of the time to describe Jesus' healing touch.

The word *therapeuo* sounds very much like the English word *therapy* and is precisely where it was derived. This Greek word *therapeuo*, translated as "healing," means *therapy*. It denotes *a healing touch that requires corresponding actions*. Imagine a physical therapist instructing a patient to move a certain way to perform a particular action to cooperate with healing. That is the idea behind this word. This type of healing power — *therapeuo* — requires cooperation.

When Jesus healed the man with the withered hand, Jesus required him to "stretch forth" his hand (*see* Mark 3:5). He was required to do something in cooperation with the healing power of God. Similarly, when Jesus healed the man who had been paralyzed for 38 years, Jesus told him, "Get up, and pick up your matt" (*see* Mark 2:11). Faith was required for this man to actually "get up." In other words, "Cooperate with God's healing power. If you *do* something in cooperation with the healing power released, it will result in a miraculous healing touch in your body."

Whenever this word *therapeuo* appears in the gospels, it describes Jesus releasing healing power, but requiring the recipient to participate — necessitating corresponding actions. So when we pray for the sick, it's important for us to instruct the individual to do something — to cooperate with God's healing power — so that the healing power of God is released.

Matthew documented the healing ministry of Jesus from its very inception. Matthew 4:23-25 records, "And Jesus went about all Galilee, teaching in their synagogues, and preaching the gospel of the kingdom, and healing all manner of sickness and all manner of disease among the people. And his fame went throughout all Syria: and they brought unto him all sick people that were taken with divers diseases and torments, and those which were possessed with devils, and those which were lunatick and those that had palsy; and he healed them. And there followed him great multitudes of people from Galilee, and from Decapolis, and from Jerusalem, and from Judaea, and from beyond Jordan."

Verse 23 begins, "And Jesus went about all Galilee *teaching* in their synagogues, and *preaching*." The word "teaching" is a participle expressing a continuous action. In other words, "Jesus went about all Galilee *teaching, teaching, teaching*." The word "preaching" is also a participle, indicating that Jesus also "went about Galilee *preaching, preaching, preaching*."

This verse continues, "...and preaching the gospel of the kingdom and *healing* all manner of sickness and all manner of disease among the people." The word "healing" is that same Greek word *therapeuo*. Jesus was touching people, speaking to people, and requiring them to do something physically. This word *therapeuo* indicates Jesus was taking time with the people He was praying for — He was *ministering* to them. He was healing (*therapying*) all manner of sickness and all manner of disease.

All Manner of Sickness

The phrase "all manner" in Matthew 4:23 is from the Greek word *poikilos*, which describes *many different kinds of sickness and disease*. And the word "sickness" here is the Greek word *nosos*. It describes *a terminal condition for which there is no natural cure*. In the pagan world at that time, it was the belief that if someone had *nosos* — a "sickness" — it was the result of evil spirits. It was believed that sickness of this particular type was created by evil or demonic spirits.

These individuals also believed that there was no remedy for it, and for that reason, it was considered *terminal*. But when Jesus arrived on the scene, that which was deemed *terminal* suddenly became *healable*. Jesus would heal — *therapeuo* — the sick, releasing the power of God and working with them to cooperate physically so they would be healed.

All Manner of Disease

Again, Matthew 4:23 says, "And Jesus went about all Galilee, teaching in their synagogues, and preaching the gospel of the kingdom, and healing all manner of sickness and all manner of *disease* among the people." The word for "disease" here is from the Greek word *malakian*, and it has a very different meaning than the Greek word *nosos*, translated as "sickness."

This word *malakian*, translated as "disease," describes *a crippling or debilitating form of sickness; a weakness.* The person afflicted by "disease" — *malakian* — is *crippled* or *debilitated.* This individual is alive but unable to function in life; in some way, he or she has been impaired or weakened, perhaps in his or her muscles, nerves, or bones.

So as Jesus went throughout the land continually preaching and teaching, He was therapying all manner of terminal sickness — *nosos* — and crippling diseases — *malakian* — among the people.

The Rumor of Jesus Christ

Jesus did so many of these miraculous events that the Bible says, "And his *fame* went throughout all Syria: and they brought unto him all sick people that were taken with divers diseases and torments, those which were possessed with devils, and those which were lunatick, and those that had the palsy; and he healed them" (Matthew 4:24).

The word "fame" is the Greek word *akoe*, which is also the Greek word for *ear.* The *ears* of the people in this region *were literally ringing with information about Jesus.* Everyone was talking about the miraculous healing ministry of Jesus. One translation for this word "fame" uses the word *rumor*: "And the *rumor* — *akoe* — of Jesus…" This Greek word *akoe* is a picture of *people's ears filled with information.* For these sick people, their *ears were filled with the rumors* of the accounts of people being healed.

Even though doctors could diagnose the sicknesses and diseases, they could not provide the medication to heal most of them. These people were really sick and had no hope. But Jesus began healing — *therapying* — the sick. Even those with terminal diseases and those physically crippled or debilitated were recovering. The healing ministry was literally *ringing in the ears* of the population.

This verse goes on to say, "…and they *brought* unto him *all* sick people…." The word "brought" is the Greek word *phero*, which means *to physically carry*. These people were so sick they were unable to walk on their own to hear Jesus, so they were physically carried to Him by friends and loved ones. And this verse also says that not just some, but "all" the sick people were brought to Jesus. In Greek, the word "all" is *panta*, and it is an *all-encompassing word*. It means *everyone; no one was excluded* from the healing touch of Jesus.

And again we come to the word "sick" in this passage, but here, the word "sick" is a translation of the Greek word *astheneia*, which generally describes *a person who is frail in health*. It pictures *one who is feeble, fragile, faint, incapacitated, disabled, or simply in such poor health that it would be unthinkable to transport this individual* because he or she is *too physically weak to travel*. And *astheneia*, translated "sick" or "sickness," generally described *all kinds of sicknesses and diseases, including financial need.* There was no category of sickness that was not included.

Those Tormented Were Healed

Matthew 4:24 then continues to describe those who were brought to Jesus saying, "…all sick people that were taken with divers *diseases* and *torments*…." The word "diseases," however, is not included in the original Greek — it was supplied by the translators. In the Greek translation, the verse simply states, "…all sick people that were taken with *divers torments.*"

The Greek word for "torments" is *basanos*, and it describes *one that is tormented* or *one that is afflicted*. This is the purpose of the enemy — he wants to steal our joy, steal our time and finances, destroy our relationships, and take our lives by tormenting us with physical sickness.

Included in the list of "all," which was *everyone; no one was excluded,* that were brought to Jesus were "…those which were possessed with devils, and those which were lunatick." The Greek literally says, "Those that were demonized, those that were lunatick." Many people had been dabbling in the occult and celebrating particular moon feasts and events related to the solar system. The people described in this passage were sick because they were dabbling in the occult.

This brings us to "… those that had the palsy." The word "palsy" refers to those who were paralyzed, and Jesus *healed* — *therapeuo* — them. And when Jesus released *therapeuo* power — healing power — He expected the person receiving that power to respond in faith to that miracle-working power.

The Bible goes on to say, "And there followed him great multitudes of people from Galilee, and from Decapolis, and from Jerusalem and from Judea, and from beyond Jordan" (Matthew 4:25). The phrase "there followed him" in Greek means *they habitually followed him*. They became *addicted* to the ministry of Jesus because it was good news — the sick could feel well, and the demon-possessed could be free. Jesus' message of healing was the best news they had ever heard! And because Jesus is the same yesterday, today, and forever, it's good news for us too!

Carried to Jesus

Mark 1:32-34 says, "And at even, when the sun did set, they *brought* unto him all that were diseased, and them that were possessed with devils. And all the city was gathered together at the door. And he healed many that were sick of divers diseases, and cast out many devils; and suffered not the devils to speak, because they knew him."

The word "brought" in Mark 1:32 is the same Greek word we found in Matthew 4:24. It is the Greek word *phero*, meaning *physically carried*. Again, it describes people who were so physically afflicted they were unable to walk in their own strength to hear Jesus' message. Because of their physical condition, friends carried — *phero* — them to Jesus.

"…When the sun did set, they brought unto him *all* that were *diseased…*" (Mark 1:32). Just as recorded in Matthew 4, the word "all" means *everyone; no one was excluded*. It denotes *everyone* in that particular town, *everyone* in that region, and *everyone* that had been afflicted. And *everyone* in this instance included those "that were diseased." The word "diseased" here are the Greek words *echo kakos*. It is a compound word of the word *echo*, which means *to have something*, and the word *kakos*, which describes *something bad or really vile*. When *echo* and *kakos* are compounded, it describes those who are *miserably afflicted* or *extremely sick*. It pictures *those in the final stages of the disease*. One expositor describes the condition of these people as being in the *final stage of their condition* as if this sickness was something *terminal*.

We learned in Matthew 4:24 that the rumors of Jesus were preceding Him, so large gatherings surrounding Jesus were common. Mark continues, "...and them that were possessed with devils. And all the city was gathered together at the door" (Mark 1:32-33). *"All* the city..." — meaning *every person* in the city had gathered to see what Jesus was doing.

The Bible says, "And He *healed* many that were sick of divers diseases and cast out many devils" (Mark 1:34). The word "healed" in this verse is again the Greek word *therapeuo*. Jesus didn't merely lay hands on the sick and diseased and expect the recipient to do nothing. When Jesus released a healing word, He would also exhort, *"Now, stretch out your hand. Move your feet. Do what you could not previously do. Do something to release the power of God."*

Jesus healed — *therapeuo* — those who were brought to Him with any form of sickness or disease. The release of God's healing power combined with the recipient's actions resulted in a miraculous touch. And verse 34 states that Jesus healed "many." In Greek, the word "many" is *pollous*, and it describes *a great number* or *vast multitudes*. This verse also says He healed many that were sick of *divers diseases*. The word translated here as "disease" is the Greek word *nosos*, which again means *those who were terminally ill*. Jesus healed those who had terminal conditions for which there was no known natural cure and no hope of recuperation.

Forcibly Evicting Demons

Mark 1:34 concludes, "And he healed many that were sick of divers diseases, and *cast out* many devils; and suffered not the devils to speak, because they knew him." The phrase "cast out" is the Greek word *ekballo*, which means to *forcibly evict*; *to throw out*; *to cast out*; *to expel*; *to drive out*; or *to kick out*. Historically, it was used to describe a nation that forcibly deported lawbreakers from its borders. Jesus came head-to-head with demons and *forcibly evicted them* from the people. And Mark 1:39 says, "And he was preaching in their synagogues throughout all Galilee, and *casting out* demons." Again, the Greek word *ekballo* is used. Jesus *forcibly evicted* those demon spirits.

When Jesus was on the scene, He *therapied* the sick — He released the power of God requiring people to cooperate, and as they did, they were set free from all manner of physical ailments and diseases. Thousands of people were healed when they encountered Jesus. And that same miraculous healing power is still available to us today.

Remember, "Jesus is the same yesterday, to day, and for ever" (Hebrews 13:8). If it was His will to heal then, it is His will to still heal today, and He will still heal tomorrow. If you are struggling with any kind of sickness or disease, you can be confident that it is emphatically the will of God for Jesus to heal you today!

STUDY QUESTIONS

Study to shew thyself approved unto God, a workman that needeth not to be ashamed, rightly dividing the word of truth.
— 2 Timothy 2:15

1.   What are the two main Greek words describing the healing ministry of Jesus and how do they differ from one another?
2.   What are the differences between the Greek words *nosos* and *malakian* as described in this lesson?

PRACTICAL APPLICATION

But be ye doers of the word, and not hearers only,
deceiving your own selves.
— James 1:22

1.   There was no sickness, disease, or condition Jesus encountered that He did not heal or cure when the recipient cooperated with God's healing power. Cite two examples of individuals in the Bible who were healed and how they cooperated with God's healing power. What can you or those you are praying for do to release faith and to receive the healing power of God?
2.   Jesus took time with people. Describe the value of how He ministered *therapy* (*therapeuo*). Why was this approach so effective? Why is a corresponding action so necessary to secure lasting results?

TOPIC

Exactly 'How' Did Jesus Heal the Sick?

SCRIPTURES

1. **John 21:25** — And there are also many other things which Jesus did, the which, if they should be written every one, I suppose that even the world itself could not contain the books that should be written. Amen.

2. **Matthew 4:23-25** — And Jesus went about all Galilee, teaching in their synagogues, and preaching the gospel of the kingdom, and healing all manner of sickness and all manner of disease among the people. And his fame went throughout all Syria: and they brought unto him all sick people that were taken with divers diseases and torments, and those which were possessed with devils, and those which were lunatick, and those that had the palsy; and he healed them. And there followed him great multitudes of people from Galilee, and from Decapolis, and from Jerusalem, and from Judaea, and from beyond Jordan.

3. **Mark 1:32-34** — And at even, when the sun did set, they brought unto him all that were diseased, and them that were possessed with devils. And all the city was gathered together at the door. And he healed many that were sick of divers diseases, and cast out many devils; and suffered not the devils to speak, because they knew him.

4. **Mark 1:39** — And he preached in their synagogues throughout all Galilee, and cast out devils.

5. **Luke 4:40** — Now when the sun was setting, all they that had any sick with divers diseases brought them unto him; and he laid hands on every one of them, and healed them.

6. **Luke 5:15** — But so much the more went there a fame abroad of him: and great multitudes came together to hear, and to be healed by him of their infirmities.

7. **John 4:45** — Then when he was come into Galilee, the Galilaeans received him, having seen all the things that he did at Jerusalem at the feast: for they also went unto the feast.

8. **Hebrews 13:8** — Jesus Christ the same yesterday, and to day, and for ever.

GREEK WORDS

1. "healing" — **θεραπεύω** (*therapeuo*): therapy; a healing touch that requires corresponding actions; primarily used to describe the healing ministry of Jesus

2. "sickness" — **νόσος** (*nosos*): a terminal condition for which there is no known natural cure; in the ancient world, it especially described spirit-induced illnesses; this type of disease held no hope of recuperation; an unalterable, irreversible, incurable, permanent condition

3. "disease" — **μαλακία** (*malakian*): a crippling or debilitating form of sickness; weakness

4. "fame" — **ἀκοή** (*akoe*): an ear; ears ringing or filled with information and news; hence, rumors or stories

5. "sickness" — **ἀσθενεία** (*astheneia*): an all-encompassing term for all types of sickness and disease; describes a person who is frail in health; one so physically weak that he is unable to travel; one who is feeble, fragile, faint, incapacitated, disabled, or simply in such poor health that it would be unthinkable to transport him; shut in or homebound; can also mean to be in financial need

6. "torments" — **βάσανος** (*basanos*): from the root word (*basano*): describes one who is tormented or one who is afflicted

7. "lunatick" — **σεληνιάζομαι** (*seleniadzomai*): moonstruck; a sickness resulting from dabbling in the occult

8. "palsy" — **παραλυτικός** (*paralutikos*): those that were paralyzed; lame; bedfast

9. "brought" — **φέρω** (*phero*): to physically carry

10. "diseased" — **ἔχω κακός** (*echo kakos*): compound of *echo* meaning to have something, and *kakos* means something bad, really vile; compounded, *echo kakos* means miserably afflicted; extremely sick; in the last stage of their condition

11. "cast out" — **ἐκβάλλω** (*ekballo*): compound word from *ek* meaning out, and *ballo*, means to throw; compounded, means to forcibly evict; to throw out; to cast out; to expel; to drive out; to kick out; historically, it was used to describe a nation that forcibly deported lawbreakers from its borders

12. "seen" — ὁράω (*horao*): to know something from personal observation, not from secondhand information; to see; to behold; to perceive; a scrutinizing look; to look with the intent to examine; an eyeful

13. "did" — ποιέω (*poieo*): a creative touch; healings of a creative nature; to do; to make; to create

SYNOPSIS

John was summing up his gospel in John 21:25 when he wrote, "And there are also many other things which Jesus did, the which, *if* they should be written every one, I suppose that even the world itself could not contain the books that should be written. Amen." The word "if" in this passage implies *it cannot be done*. It was not possible to write every healing, every miracle, and all that Jesus did while He was on earth. If it were possible, and John said it was not, the books written could not be contained!

The four gospels were written to document the life of Jesus, but according to this verse in John, only a very few of those events were actually recorded in the gospels. Jesus ministered for three and a half years while He walked on this earth as a man, and it is projected that only 27 days of Jesus' entire life were documented. Think about it: It took four gospels to record 27 days of Jesus' life on earth! What do you suppose Jesus did on the other days that were *not* documented? Thanks to the gospel writers, we have some snapshots of Jesus' life on earth, but there is so much more that was not documented.

The emphasis of this lesson:

Healing is evidenced in the gospels and not one instance of sickness, disease or infirmity was exempt. Vast multitudes of people who were sick or diseased came to Jesus, and not one sickness represented in those multitudes was exempt from the healing power of God!

Cooperating With God's Healing Power

The four gospels provide specific events in the lives of individuals that were healed by Jesus. We can read about Jairus' daughter (*see* Mark 5:21-43; Luke 8:40-42,49-56), the woman with the issue of blood (*see* Mark 5:25-34; Luke 8:43-48), and the ten lepers (*see* Luke 17:11-19) — all are concrete and very notable events. However, in addition to these specific recorded events of healings and miracles, there are passages indicating that thousands more healings and miracles were not specifically recorded.

Mark states that Jesus "healed many" (*see* Mark 1:34) or healed *vast multitudes* according to the Greek. Vast multitudes of people received a miraculous touch from Jesus while He walked this earth, and the majority of those healings were identified as the Greek word *therapeuo*, meaning as Jesus released healing power, *it was required that the recipient cooperate* by responding with a physical action such as stretching forth a hand, walking, or "rising up and picking up the mat."

It's important to note that Jesus' healing ministry was not rushed — He took His time with each person. When Jesus released God's healing power, He would say to the person desiring to be healed, *"Now, let's do something to cooperate…move your hand…move your back…do what you couldn't do before."* It was when the recipient began to act and respond by faith that they discovered they had been healed.

So why don't we see more manifestations of God's healing today? One reason may be because we often do not pray as Jesus did. We may pray a prayer in faith — or we may even pray in the name of Jesus and with authority. But we fall short when we fail to ask the recipient to *do something* after we have prayed for them.

If we pray for a person's hand to be healed, but don't ask them to move that hand after prayer, we fall short. If we pray for someone who is deaf in one ear and do not have them test that ear after praying for them, again, we fall short. So, if we pray for someone who needs healing for their foot, we need to have them try to move that foot after we pray. If a person has had back problems and we pray for their back to be healed, we need to ask them to try to stretch, twist, or bend over. Whoever we are praying for in the area of healing, we need to ask them to do something *to cooperate* with God's healing power.

In the majority of the healing cases cited in Jesus' healing ministry, Jesus therapied — *therapeuo* — those He prayed for. He encouraged and expected the cooperation of those He prayed for, and we should do the same today.

Healing All — Nothing and No One Excluded

Revisiting Matthew 4:23-25: "And Jesus went about all Galilee, teaching in their synagogues, and preaching the gospel of the kingdom and healing all manner of *sickness* and all manner of disease among the people. And his fame went throughout all Syria: and they brought unto him all sick people that were taken with divers diseases and torments, and those which were possessed with devils, and those which were lunatick, and those that had the palsy; and he healed them. And there followed him great multitudes of people from Galilee, and from Decapolis, and from Jerusalem, and from Judaea, and from beyond Jordan."

As Jesus went throughout the lands, He was teaching, and He was preaching, and He was healing. The Word confirms that Jesus healed *all* manner of sickness and *all* manner of disease that existed among the people. Again, the Greek word for "sickness" in verse 23 is *nosos*, and it describes *a terminal condition for which there is no natural cure*. These were people who had no hope for healing, but when they encountered Jesus, they received hope because Jesus had power to reverse terminal conditions!

Jesus was going around healing "all manner of sickness" — *nosos* — terminal conditions for which there was no cure, and "all manner of *disease*." The word "disease" is translated from the Greek word *malakian*. It describes those who are *crippled or physically debilitated*. These people were living and breathing, but they could not function because their muscles, nerves, or skeletal structure had been affected.

Verse 24 goes on to say, "And his *fame* went throughout all Syria: and they brought unto him all sick people that were taken with divers diseases and torments, and those which were possessed with devils, and those which were lunatick, and those that had the palsy; and he healed them." The word "fame" is the Greek word *akoe*, which means *ear*. The *ears* of the people in that region were tingling and buzzing with information about the healings and miracles Jesus was performing. The doctors may have been able to diagnose their conditions, but they could not heal them. So when people heard the good news that Jesus could heal them, they had hope because they were hearing the answer to their "incurable" condition.

This Greek phrase "…and they *brought* unto him…" describes people who needed physical healing but had to be carried by others to Jesus because they were so critically ill they were unable to walk to Jesus unassisted.

This verse also states, "...they brought unto him [Jesus] *all* sick people...." This Greek word for "all" — *panta* — means *no one was excluded*. It means anyone in that neighborhood or city or region who was sick came to see Jesus. *Every* person who was sick was brought to Jesus to be healed!

The word for "sick" in this passage describes *every type of ailment; those miserably afflicted, and extremely sick.* In this crowd that gathered, every ailment, every sickness, every disease, even those in the final stages of the illness, *everything* known to man was represented in the people that came before Him. And the word "torments," translated from the Greek word *basanos*, describes the effect of sickness and disease — stolen health and wholeness — sent by the devil to torment those with sickness and ailments.

Even those "...possessed with devils and those which were *lunatick*" were brought before Jesus. In the Greek, "lunatick" means *moonstruck*. It describes individuals that were dabbling in the occult and as a result had become afflicted with demon spirits. And finally, Matthew 4:24 includes those "...that had the *palsy*" among those who Jesus healed. The Greek meaning for the word "palsy" describes those that were *paralyzed.* Jesus healed them *all!*

So what did Jesus do with the *nosos* — the terminally sick? What did He do with those that were *malakian* — physically debilitated or crippled? What did He do with those who were *astheneia* — so frail from sickness they were homebound? What did He do with those who were tormented by physical affliction? What did Jesus do with those possessed with demons because they had dabbled in the occult? Matthew tells us Jesus dealt with all of these the same way — He healed (*therapeuo*) them. Jesus released the power of God to all who came, and He required them to respond physically in some way.

The result of Jesus' healing ministry is found in Matthew 4:25: "And there followed him great multitudes of people from Galilee, and from Decapolis, and from Jerusalem, and from Judaea, and from beyond Jordan." According to the Greek, a better translation is, "And there followed Him *habitually* great multitudes of people...." A vast multitude of people, not wanting to lose sight of Jesus, followed Him constantly.

Mark 1:32-34 sums up the ministry of Jesus. "And at even, when the sun did set, they brought unto him all that were diseased, and them that were possessed with devils. And all the city was gathered together at the door.

And he healed many that were sick of divers diseases, and cast out many devils; and suffered not the devils to speak, because they knew him."

Once again, we see the word "brought," which is a translation from the Greek word *phero*, meaning that friends and family *physically carried* those who could not get to Jesus on their own. And not just a few were brought to Jesus — they "brought *all* unto him that were diseased...." This little word "all" means *every, nothing excluded*. And the phrase "...that were diseased" is from the Greek words *echo kako* and refers to *those who were in a bad or foul way, those in the final stages of their affliction; those drawing their last breath*. Every kind of sickness and disease and everyone who was sick — no one and no kind of sickness, no matter how severe, was excluded from the healing touch of Jesus.

Verse 33 continues, "And all the city was gathered together at the door." You can imagine what kind of excitement was stirred up by these healings. This event brought everyone from the city to see for themselves the great and wonderous things that were happening.

"And he *healed* many that were sick of divers diseases, and cast out many devils..." (Mark 1:34). Once again, the Greek word for "healed" here is *therapeuo*. Jesus released the power of God and required the people He prayed for to respond physically in some way. And in this way, Jesus "healed" or *therapied* many. The word "many" is from the Greek word *pollous*, and it describes *a vast multitude* or *a great number* of people who were sick.

Evicting Demons

Mark 1:34 continues, "...and *cast out* many devils." The same Greek word is used in this passage as we saw in Matthew 4 for "cast out." It is the Greek word *ekballo*, meaning *to forcibly evict*. Just as we would evict an unwelcomed person from our property, Jesus evicted demons out of people. He refused to allow those demons to remain in people who wanted to be free of them.

The phrase "cast out," the Greek word *ekballo*, is found again just a few verses later in Mark 1:39. It says, "And he preached in their synagogues throughout all Galilee, and *cast out* devils." Jesus never hesitated to *forcibly evict* those demons from people who were tormented by their presence.

Great Multitudes

Luke also recorded the healing ministry of Jesus. "Now when the sun was setting, all they that had any *sick* with divers diseases brought them unto him; and he laid his hands on every one of them, and healed them" (Luke 4:40). The word "sick" here is the Greek word *astheneia*, which is *an all-encompassing term that includes every sort of physical illness, ailment, or sickness.* Again, no illness was exempt from the healing power of Jesus Christ.

Verse 40 concludes, "...He laid his hands on every one of them, and healed them." Notice, Jesus first laid His hands on those brought to Him to deliver the power of God, but secondly, He required those He prayed for to "do" something.

Luke, a doctor by trade, explicitly said of Jesus in this passage, "He *healed* them." Once again, the Greek word *therapeuo* is translated as "healed." As has been highlighted previously, this word for healing — *therapeuo* — describes a partnership between the power of God and the cooperation of the recipient. Jesus prayed the prayer of faith, released the power of God, and then immediately asked them to do something: "*Stretch out your hand. Bend over. Move your leg. Do something you couldn't do before.*" In other words, Jesus said, "*Cooperate with the healing power that has been released in you.*"

And Luke confirms the magnitude of people seeking out and receiving the power of God: "But so much the more went there a fame abroad of him; and *great multitudes* came together to hear, and to be healed by Him of their infirmities" (Luke 5:15). Why did great multitudes come together? They came together to hear. And they came to hear the message of Jesus so they could be healed — *therapeuo* — of their *infirmities*. "Infirmities" here is a translation of the same Greek word *astheneia*, also translated as "sickness." It is *an all-encompassing term for all types of sickness and disease,* and it describes *those in such poor health, it was unthinkable to transport them.* No one was exempt or excluded. They simply had to cooperate with God's healing power.

Having Seen

Looking again at John 4:45, it says, "Then when he was come into Galilee, the Galilaeans received him, having *seen* all the things that he did at Jerusalem at the feast: for they also went unto the feast." The word "seen" is the Greek word *horao*, meaning *to know something by personal observation or experience.* This tells us this was not secondhand information. In other words, John said, "*This is no longer hearsay information, but I know this based on what I have seen with my own eyes and based on my own experience.*"

The Galileans who were present in Jerusalem saw many healings and miracles throughout the ministry of Jesus. Verse 45 says, "…the Galilaeans received him, having seen all the things that he *did* at Jerusalem." The word translated as "did" in this verse is the Greek word *poieo*, and it describes *a creative touch* or *healings of a creative nature.* This was another whole level of miracle power Jesus operated and moved in. This type of miracle healing involved the creation of arms where none existed or eyes being created where there was blindness. Jesus moved in creative power to — *poieo* — *do, make,* or *create* what had never existed before.

Each of the four gospels — Matthew, Mark, Luke, and John — describe the fact that even though there were specific documented healings of individuals, so many were healed in the crowds that came or were brought to Jesus, it was impossible to document them all. But it is a mistake to say, "*Wow! It's so amazing the number of people Jesus healed of sickness and disease! It's amazing…but that happened 2,000 years ago.*" Don't make that mistake. Hebrews 13:8 emphatically states, "Jesus Christ the same yesterday, and to day, and for ever."

In the Greek, this is a mathematical equation describing the unchanging nature of Jesus Christ. He is absolutely unchanging. He is completely consistent. What He *was* and what He *is*, is what He *will be*. If He healed in the past, He is healing today. If He worked miracles in the past, He is working miracles today. He is the same yesterday, today, and forever!

STUDY QUESTIONS

Study to shew thyself approved unto God, a workman that needeth not to be ashamed, rightly dividing the word of truth.
— 2 Timothy 2:15

1. Describe how sickness and disease "steal" from those afflicted with sickness and disease.
2. Describe the meaning of the Greek word *poieo* and how it relates to the healing ministry of Jesus.

PRACTICAL APPLICATION

> But be ye doers of the word, and not hearers only,
> deceiving your own selves.
> — James 1:22

1. Hebrews 13:8 assures that Jesus Christ is the same — yesterday, today, and forever. Describe how the knowledge of this truth enables you to better receive healing for yourself personally or minister healing to others.

2. Knowing Jesus is the same yesterday, today, and forever, and that His miraculous healing power is still available to us today, what can you do specifically to allow the Lord to manifest His healing power through you?

LESSON 3

TOPIC

The Use of 'Therapy' in Jesus' Ministry

SCRIPTURES

1. **Matthew 4:23-25** — And Jesus went about all Galilee, teaching in their synagogues, and preaching the gospel of the kingdom, and healing all manner of sickness and all manner of disease among the people. And his fame went throughout all Syria: and they brought unto him all sick people that were taken with divers diseases and torments, and those which were possessed with devils, and those which were lunatick, and those that had the palsy; and he healed them. And there followed him great multitudes of people from Galilee, and from Decapolis, and from Jerusalem, and from Judaea, and from beyond Jordan.

2. **John 5:1-4** — After this there was a feast of the Jews; and Jesus went up to Jerusalem. Now there is at Jerusalem by the sheep *market* [gate] a pool, which is called in the Hebrew tongue Bethesda, having five porches. In these lay a great multitude of impotent folk, of blind, halt, withered, waiting for the moving of the water. For an angel went down at a certain season into the pool, and troubled the water: who-

soever then first after the troubling of the water stepped in was made whole of whatsoever disease he had.

3. **John 5:5,6** — And a certain man was there, which had an infirmity thirty and eight years. When Jesus saw him lie, and knew that he had been now a long time in that case, he saith unto him, Wilt thou be made whole?

4. **John 5:7-10** — The impotent man answered him, Sir, I have no man, when the water is troubled, to put me into the pool: but while I am coming, another steppeth down before me. Jesus said unto him, Rise, take up thy bed, and walk. And immediately the man was made whole, and took up his bed, and walked: and on the same day was the sabbath. The Jews therefore said unto him that was cured, It is the sabbath day: it is not lawful for thee to carry thy bed.

5. **Hebrews 13:8** — Jesus Christ the same yesterday, and to day, and for ever.

GREEK WORDS

1. "sickness" — ἀσθενεία (*astheneia*): an all-encompassing term for all types of sickness and disease; describes a person who is frail in health; one so physically weak that he is unable to travel; one who is feeble, fragile, faint, incapacitated, disabled, or simply in such poor health that it would be unthinkable to transport him; shut in or homebound; can also mean to be in financial need

2. "sickness" — νόσος (*nosos*): a terminal condition for which there is no known natural cure; in the ancient world, it especially described spirit-induced illnesses; this type of disease held no hope of recuperation; an unalterable, irreversible, incurable, permanent condition

3. "disease" — μαλακία (*malakian*): a crippling or debilitating form of sickness; weakness

4. "lunatick" — σεληνιάζομαι (*seleniadzomai*): moonstruck; a sickness resulting from dabbling in the occult

5. "palsy" — παραλυτικός (*paralutikos*): paralyzed; lame; bedfast

6. "healing" — θεραπεύων (*therapeuo*): therapy; a healing touch that requires corresponding actions; primarily used to describe the healing ministry of Jesus

7. "pool" — κολυμβήθρα (*kolumbethra*): a swimming pool; a highly sophisticated, beautifully developed place

8. "lay" — **περίκειμαι** (*katakeimai*): people stacked on top of people

9. "impotent" — **ἀσθενέία** (*astheneia*): an all-encompassing term for all types of sickness and disease

10. "time" — **χρόνος** (*chronos*): time; specifically, a long time; here, a chronic condition

11. "cured" — **θεραπεύω** (*therapeuo*): to serve; to cure; pictures a healing touch that requires corresponding actions; therapy; primarily used to describe the healing ministry of Jesus

SYNOPSIS

Each of the four gospels — Matthew, Mark, Luke, and John — touch on the healing ministry of Jesus. As He went about preaching and teaching, Jesus healed *every* sickness (*astheneia*) and disease (*malakian*) imaginable that was present in the vast multitudes of people who followed Him. From the frailest in health to those crippled or debilitated, there was no sickness exempt from the healing power of Jesus Christ. Friends and families brought their loved ones who were sick (*nosos*) with incurable diseases to the One they had been hearing about.

Jesus healed (*therapeuo*) many, and He also took authority over the devil, casting out (*ekballo*) demons and restoring those who were tormented (*basanos*) and diseased (*echo kakos*). And we know that Jesus is the same yesterday, today, and forever (*see* Hebrews 13:8). What He did for *all* then, He does for *all* today.

The emphasis of this lesson:

Pools, that had at one time been opulent respites for the wealthy, had become a place where the sick watched and waited for the waters in the pool to move in hopes of receiving healing. In this setting, Jesus healed a man who had been waiting 38 years to be healed!

A Pool by the Sheep Market

In John's gospel, we find another vivid example of healing — *therapeuo* — that was prevalent in Jesus' ministry. "After this there was a feast of the Jews; and Jesus went up to Jerusalem. Now there is at Jerusalem by the sheep market a pool, which is called in the Hebrew tongue Bethesda, having five porches. In these lay a great multitude of impotent folk, of blind, halt, withered, waiting for the moving of the water. For an angel went down at a certain season into the pool, and troubled the water: whosoever then first after troubling the water stepped in was made whole of whatsoever disease he had" (John 5:1-4).

The information surrounding Bethesda is historically accurate: "Now there is at Jerusalem by the sheep *market* a pool" (John 5:2). In the *King James Version*, the word "market" is italicized, meaning it does not appear in the Greek: the translators added the word "market." The Greek word is *pule*, which describes *a gate*. Instead of a "sheep *market*," the correct translation is "sheep *gate*." This gate was located on the eastern side of the temple where the sheep were brought in for the sacrifices.

The Greek word for "pool" in verse 2 is *kolumbethra*. The word *kolumbethra* describes *a swimming pool*. Specifically, *a highly sophisticated, beautifully developed place*. The word "pool" is found only one other time in the New Testament. In John 9:7 and 11, this same Greek word for "pool" — *kolumbethra* — is used to describe the Pool of Siloam. In both examples, the Pool of Bethesda and the Pool of Siloam, are descriptions of very beautiful and luxurious places.

The Pool of Siloam was impressive and very well developed — it was not simply a hole in the ground. The sides of the pool were covered with marble and stone. There were steps leading into the pool from every side. The veranda — the patio surrounding the pool — was completely covered with beautiful masonry and stonework. It was a luxurious, well-developed, sophisticated place.

John 5:2 tells us that there were *five porches* surrounding the Pool of Bethesda. The Greek word for "porches" is *stoas*, and the Greek word for "five" is *pente*. Compounded, the word *pentestoas* describes *five, covered porches or colonnades*. In the location of these colonnades, beautiful mosaics, statues, and artwork could be found. The porches were covered with terracotta tiles on the surface, and the sidewalks were typically covered with mosaics. Because of its beauty, many people congregated at the pool. The fact that there were five *stoas* or colonnades indicates why so many were drawn to this pool. Similar pools had only one stoa, which was impressive, but imagine the magnificence of this pool that had five stoas!

The name Bethesda was not the original name for this pool. According to the Greek, it was named this by the Hebrews, and was considered a nickname. Bethesda was the name ascribed to it by sick people who came to this place with the hope of being healed.

The Pool of Bethesda was located very near to the temple and near the Sheep Gate on the eastern side. The waters contained in this pool were mineral waters and considered to be curative and very good for overall health. Similar to a spa in our day, in order to visit this pool, there were high fees attached to bathing in these mineral springs or mineral waters. The Pool of Bethesda was considered to be one of the prime locations in the city of Jerusalem. It was located close to the temple, therefore, many educated people, even those in the priesthood, frequented this pool. After a long day of work, the elite educated people would dine under the five stoas — the covered colonnades. It was the place for the intelligentsia of this region. It has even been referred to as the "country club" of Jerusalem — a well-developed, sophisticated place.

However, at the time described in John Chapter 5, the elite had abandoned this place for some reason. Some have speculated that perhaps the water had begun to lose its medicinal powers, therefore, the wealthy became uninterested in it and abandoned it as a desired destination. After the wealthy left the place, the sick people began to occupy it and they nicknamed it "The House of Mercy." Why? Because this is the place where mercy was poured out. The word *bethesda* literally means *the place where mercy is outpoured.* Those seeking healing in this place knew something supernatural was happening.

Waiting for the Waters To Move

The passage in John reveals that from time-to-time an angel would stir the waters at the Pool of Bethesda and the first sick person to enter the water as it was stirred would be supernaturally healed. John 5:1-3 says, "After this there was a feast of the Jews; and Jesus went up to Jerusalem. Now there is at Jerusalem by the sheep market (*gate*) a pool, which is called in the Hebrew tongue Bethesda, having five porches. In these lay a great multitude of impotent folk, of blind, halt, withered, waiting for the moving of the water."

The word translated as "lay" in verse 3 is the Greek word *katakeimai*, and it is a picture of *people stacked on top of people.* Sick individuals had gathered at this pool from all over the region. This wasn't just a *few* sick people — it was a "great multitude" of sick people that were laying everywhere in hopes of a miraculous touch from God to heal their bodies. And among this vast multitude, the Word describes those that waited as "*impotent* folk of *blind, halt,* and *withered.*"

In Greek, the word "impotent" is *astheneia* — the same word that is also translated "sick" and "diseased." *Astheneia is an all-encompassing term for all types of sickness and disease.* Again, it describes *a person who is frail in health; one who is feeble, fragile, faint, incapacitated, disabled, or simply in such poor health that it would be unthinkable to transport that person.* Those who were "blind" were also found near the Pool of Bethesda. The word "blind" in Greek is a translation of the word *tuphlos,* which means *opaque, as if smokey, darkened by smoke; to be physically or mentally blind; unable to see.* It could also denote someone who *physically had no eyes with which to see.*

In addition to the impotent and blind, the "halt" and "withered" waited by the pool. The word "halt" is translated from the Greek word *cholos,* which refers to *those who are lame or crippled; deprived of a limb or limbs.* The term "withered" means to be *deprived of natural strength.* It *pictures those whose physical limbs are shrunk, wasted, or withered away.* It also describes *people who are drying up* or *have given up on life and have lost hope.* To be "withered" also meant that these individuals were *considered to be the non-contributors of society.*

John 5:3 tells us that these people he just described were "waiting for the moving of the water." This massive crowd of sick and diseased people who had gathered around the Pool of Bethesda were just waiting for the moving of the water in the pool. Imagine: a vast multitude of sick people lying beneath these five covered colonnades with their eyes fixed on the water in that pool.

Scripture then tells us, "For an angel went down at a certain season into the pool, and *troubled* the water: whosoever then first after the troubling of the water stepped in was made whole of whatsoever disease he had" (John 5:4). The Greek word for "troubled" in this verse is *tarasso.* But this word does not describe the normal movement of water. Instead, it depicts *a fierce agitation of water.* Some have speculated the movement of the water was the result of the wind, however, this Greek word describes *purposeful agitation, to be shaken up or troubled.* This was not the natural movement of water, but something very supernatural. All of these many, many sick and diseased people were completely focused on the water in that pool just waiting and anticipating its supernatural agitation so they could be the first one in the pool to be healed.

Waiting Thirty-Eight Years

The story continues in verse 5: "And a certain man was there, which had an infirmity thirty and eight years." When the term *a certain man* or *a certain woman* is used, it indicates that this person was living during the time the Gospel was written. The *certain man* mentioned in this passage was someone everyone knew. This man had been sick for 38 years! He was a fixture in this place. We know he had a chronic condition, but we also know he had faith. He had left his home and made a way to get to this pool and arrived in faith that he would be the first in the pool and receive his healing.

"When Jesus saw him lie, and knew that he had now been *a long time* in that case, he saith unto him, Wilt thou be made whole?" (John 5:6) The phrase "a long time" is the Greek word *chronos*, which describes *a chronic condition*. For 38 years, without a single day free of his affliction, the man lay by the pool, waiting for his chance to be the "first one in."

Jesus asked this man, "Wilt thou be made whole?" What a strange question for Jesus to ask someone who had been physically afflicted for 38 years!

For 38 years this man could not work, had no social life, and had been living with this condition as life continued to move past him. But society had changed. Education and technology had changed. If this man was suddenly made well by Jesus, it would not only affect his physical body and health, but healing would also affect his mind, his social life, and his daily life as a whole. There would be a dramatic transformation in every area of his life: He would need to get a job; He may need to learn a new trade or get an education; He would need to find a new place to live!

Jesus had asked, "Are you sure this is what you want? Do you really want to be made whole?" There are many sick and diseased people who say they want to be healed, but when presented with the opportunity to be healed, they embrace sickness instead of wholeness because the sickness has become their identity — their way of life.

But this man *did* want to be healed. "The impotent man answered him, Sir, I have no man, when the water is troubled, to put me into the pool: but while I am coming, another steppeth down before me" (John 5:7). For 38 years, others had beaten him into the troubled waters at Bethesda.

Cooperate: Rise, Take Up Your Bed, and Walk

Notice Jesus' response in verse 8: "Jesus saith unto him, Rise, take up thy bed, and walk." Jesus released the power to heal (*therapeuo*), but He required the man's participation — to rise, to take up his bed, and to walk. In faith, the afflicted man chose to cooperate with Jesus, and rose up from his place of sickness. "And immediately the man was made whole, and took up his bed, and walked: and on the same day was the sabbath" (John 5:9).

Although this man's emotional response was not recorded, verse 10 reveals the response of the religious leaders to this supernatural healing. John 5:10 says, "The Jews therefore said unto him that was *cured*, It is the sabbath day: it is not lawful for thee to carry thy bed." The Greek word for "cured" is translated from the very same word we have been studying — *therapeuo*. Even the Jewish religious leaders understood this was the manner of Jesus' healing ministry. From their perspective, they knew Jesus released some kind of power and then required the sick people to respond with an action or react in some way. It was Jesus' will for the sick to be made well then, and it's still His will for the sick to be made well today.

STUDY QUESTIONS

> Study to shew thyself approved unto God, a workman that needeth
> not to be ashamed, rightly dividing the word of truth.
> — 2 Timothy 2:15

1. What does the Greek word *tarasso* describe concerning the water in the Pool of Bethesda?

2. How did the man by the pool who had been afflicted for 38 years obtain his healing? What was this man's condition according to the Greek language?

PRACTICAL APPLICATION

> But be ye doers of the word, and not hearers only,
> deceiving your own selves.
> — James 1:22

1. What are you doing to make the healing ministry of Jesus more than just a concept, but instead, a practical reality in your life? In addition

to prayer, study, and obedient action, how are you pursuing the healing ministry of Jesus in and through your life?

2. Recount the healings you have received in your life. Do you still remember to give God thanks and to give testimony to others about God's faithfulness to you?

TOPIC

Healing Power for All Who Believe

SCRIPTURES

1. **Mark 5:21-24** — And when Jesus was passed over again by ship unto the other side, much people gathered unto him: and he was nigh unto the sea. And, behold, there cometh one of the rulers of the synagogue, Jairus by name; and when he saw him, he fell at his feet, And besought him greatly, saying, My little daughter lieth at the point of death: I pray thee, come and lay thy hands on her, that she may be healed; and she shall live. And Jesus went with him; and much people followed him, and thronged him.

2. **Mark 5:25-29,34** — And a certain woman, which had an issue of blood twelve years, And had suffered many things of many physicians, and had spent all that she had, and was nothing bettered, but rather grew worse. When she had heard of Jesus, came in the press behind, and touched his garment. For she said, If I may touch but his clothes, I shall be whole. And straightway the fountain of her blood was dried up; and she felt in her body that she was healed of that plague. ...And he said unto her, Daughter, thy faith hath made thee whole; go in peace, and be whole of thy plague.

3. **Leviticus 15:19-27** — And if a woman have an issue, and her issue in her flesh be blood, she shall be put apart seven days: and whosoever thoucheth her shall be unclean until the even. And every thing that she lieth upon in her separation shall be unclean: every thing also that she sitteth upon shall be unclean. And whosoever toucheth her bed shall wash his clothes, and bathe himself in water, and be unclean until the even. And whosoever toucheth any thing that she sat upon

shall wash his clothes, and bathe himself in water, and be unclean until the even. And if it be on her bed, or on any thing whereon she sitteth, when he toucheth it, he shall be unclean until the even. And if any man lie with her at all, and her flowers be upon him, he shall be unclean seven days; and all the bed whereon he lieth shall be unclean. And if a woman have an issue of her blood many days out of the time of her separation, or if it run beyond the time of her separation; all the days of the issue of her uncleanness shall be as the days of her separation: she shall be unclean. Every bed whereon she lieth all the days of her issue shall be unto her as the bed of her separation: and whatsoever she sitteth upon shall be unclean, as the uncleanness of her separation. And whosoever toucheth those things shall be unclean, and shall wash his clothes, and bathe himself in water, and be unclean until the even.

GREEK WORDS

1. "healing" — θεραπεύω (*therapeuo*): therapy; a healing touch that requires corresponding actions; primarily used to describe the healing ministry of Jesus

2. "much people" — ὄχλος πολύς (*ochlos polus*): a large crowd; a vast multitude; a massive crowd

3. "fell" — πίπτω (*pipto*): to collapse

4. "besought" — παρακαλέω (*parakaleo*): compound of (*para*) means alongside, and (*kaleo*) means to ask; compounded, means to beg intensely; to plead; to urge or beseech; used to depict military leaders who came alongside their troops to urge, exhort, beseech, beg, and plead with them to stand tall and face their battles bravely

5. "saved" — σώζω (*sodzo*): salvation; wholeness in every part of life; a touch of salvation that brings delivering and healing power that results in wholeness

6. "thronged" — συνθλίβω (*sunthlibo*): to press; to crush, as to crush grapes or even bones; to crush from all sides; from the root word *thlipsis*, which means great, crushing, suffocating pressure; trouble

7. "suffered" — πάθος (*pathos*): physical and mental suffering; to suffer; carries the idea of suffering, undergoing hardships, being ill-treated, or experiencing adversity; the tense means continual suffering

8. "whole" — σώζω (*sodzo*): a touch of salvation that brings delivering and healing power that results in wholeness

9. "peace" — εἰρήνη (*eirene*): the cessation of war; the end of conflict; a time of reconstruction or rebuilding

SYNOPSIS

In the last three lessons, we examined the various kinds of sickness described in the gospels. We studied how Jesus healed, and learned that in the vast majority of healings recorded, the word "heal" is the Greek word *therapeuo*, which means when Jesus released God's healing power, He expected the recipient of that healing to cooperate with it and to do something he or she may not have been able to do before.

The emphasis of this lesson:

As a vast multitude greeted Jesus at the shore, thronging him at the water's edge, Jairus appeared. And an unclean woman, afflicted with an issue of blood for twelve years, heard of the healings of Jesus and allowed faith to arise in her heart to be healed.

A Vast Multitude

There's another powerful story found in the gospel of Mark about the miraculous healing ministry of Jesus.

Mark 5:1-20 recounts Jesus' arrival in the country of the Gadarenes. When His ship landed, He was immediately met by two demon-possessed men — and Jesus cast out the demons from both. Mark mentions one demon-possessed man being present and Matthew mentions two, but these are two accounts of the same incident. In his gospel, Mark simply focused on the most dramatic case. He recorded that when this particular man was set free, he immediately began to evangelize to the entire region by sharing about what had happened to him.

After Jesus delivered these two men, He got back into His boat and returned to the other side. "And when Jesus was passed over again by ship unto the other side, *much people* gathered unto him and he was nigh unto the sea" (Mark 5:21). This verse is very important because it paints an entire picture of what was awaiting Jesus when He traveled back to the other side of the Sea of Galilee.

When His ship arrived, Jesus was greeted by "much people." The Greek word for "people" is *ochlos*, and it means *a very large crowd*. It depicts *a vast multitude of people.* But when you add the amplifier "much," the Greek word *polus*, it means this wasn't just a very large crowd — this was *a massive, enormous, almost innumerable crowd* that had formed. People had heard that Jesus' ship was returning to their side of the sea and they had gathered, waiting for His arrival.

Verse 21 of Mark 5 continues, "...and he was *nigh* unto the sea." The word "nigh" is *para*, which means *alongside*. A better translation would be, "He was alongside the sea." The crowd had grown, and they waited at the water's edge for Jesus to return. Having heard about the two demon-possessed men being set free, everyone from the city had gone down to the seashore to meet Jesus.

When Jesus disembarked from the ship, He was met by this multitude. They were pushing and shoving — everyone in the crowd wanted to touch Jesus making it very difficult for Him to get away from the water's edge. One expositor explains this moment as the picture of the crowd pushing Jesus back out into the water, ankle deep or knee deep in the water, while the crowd mercilessly tried to get to Him.

Jairus

In the midst of this growing crowd, a man emerged to speak directly to Jesus. "And, *behold*, there cometh one of the rulers of the synagogue, Jairus by name; and when he saw him, he fell at his feet" (Mark 5:22). In Greek, the word for "behold" literally means *wow*. A better translation would be "And, *wow!* There came one of the rulers of the synagogue, Jairus by name."

Jairus was very well-known in the community. He was extremely rich, intelligent, and famous. Among the people, he was viewed almost as some type of royalty. Jairus was a ruler of the synagogue and would have been dressed in magnificent regalia simply because of who he was. Everyone knew Jairus.

Verse 22 continues, "...and when he [Jairus] saw him [Jesus], he fell at his feet." Imagine the scene: A massive crowd was reaching, pushing, and jabbing just to touch Jesus, and He was having a difficult time getting to the shore because of the throng surrounding Him. Then, suddenly, from the back of the crowd, someone began yelling, "Jairus is here!" The crowd slowly began to move out of Jesus' way and to make a path that would allow Jairus to get to Jesus.

Imagine, as Jairus, with his servants at his side, walking through the crowd to the water's edge to reach Jesus. He was so desperate for a healing touch for his own daughter, Jairus fell at the feet of Jesus. The word "fell" here means literally *to collapse*.

Now at the feet of Jesus, Jairus made his plea: "And *besought* him greatly, saying, My little daughter lieth at the point of death: I pray thee, come and lay thy hands on her, that she may be healed; and she shall live" (Mark 5:23). In Greek, the word "besought" is *parakaleo*. It is a compound of the root word *para*, which means *alongside*, and *kaleo*, which means *to ask*. When these two words are compounded to form *parakaleo*, it means *to plead; to urge,* or *to beseech*. It pictures one who is *begging intensely*.

Jairus' Bold Request

From this lowly position on the ground, Jairus was probably looking up at Jesus, holding onto Him, begging and pleading. The Greek supports the translation of Jairus' lament as, "*My little daughter is in the last stage of her illness and at the point of death.*" The Bible doesn't reveal the illness this little girl had been afflicted with, but it seems it came in stages, and she was at the point of drawing her last breath.

Jairus was bold in his request. The words "I pray thee" in verse 23 don't appear in the original Greek text but were later added by the translators. In fact, Jairus made the demand, "Come and lay hands on her, that she may be *healed*; and she shall live." The word translated "healed" here is the Greek word *sodzo*, meaning *salvation*. *Sodzo* pictures *wholeness in every part of life; a touch of salvation that brings delivering and healing power that results in wholeness*. Jairus' daughter was in need of total deliverance and healing that would make her whole in every way.

How did Jesus respond to this command? Mark 5:24 says, "And Jesus went with him; and much people followed him, and thronged him." Jesus was not offended by Jairus' demand. Instead, He saw his faith and went with Jairus.

But in order for Jesus to follow Jairus, He had to walk through the vast multitude that had gathered. The crowd had made a little pathway for Jairus, but as Jesus followed him, "…much people *thronged* Him." The word "thronged" is the Greek word *sunthlibo*, which means *to press; to crush from all sides, as to crush grapes or even bones*. And this Greek word comes from the root word *thlipsis*, which means *a great, crushing, suffocating pressure*.

This was a crushing crowd — nearly suffocating Jesus as they all pressed in to get near Him. They knew the Miracle Worker, the Healer, was walking through them, and everyone was desperate to get to Him.

The Woman With an Issue of Blood

As Jesus made His way to Jairus' daughter, He encountered another person in great need of a healing touch. "And a certain woman, which had an issue of blood twelve years, And had suffered many things of many physicians, and had spent all that she had, and was nothing bettered, but rather grew worse. When she had heard of Jesus, came in the press behind, and touched his garment. For she said, If I may touch but his clothes, I shall be whole" (Mark 5:25-28).

The fact that this woman had been afflicted with an issue of blood was very serious. In addition to the physical, emotional, and financial toll on her life, she was deemed *unclean*. According to Levitical Law, as an *unclean person* she had to isolate herself and was forbidden to touch anyone. And if anyone accidentally touched her, that person would *also* be considered unclean. Furthermore, if this woman was married, she was forbidden from having a physical relationship with her husband (*see* Leviticus 15:19-27).

Levitical Law deemed this woman with an issue of blood as *unclean* — she could not be touched; she could not share a meal with others; people around her could not sit where she sat, they could not touch her clothes, nor could they touch anything that she had touched. Basically, she was completely isolated and cut off from contact with others. And this woman had suffered with this issue of blood for 12 years!

When Mark, in his gospel, described this particular woman as having an issue of blood for 12 years, it meant she had not been touched by her husband for 12 years. If she had children, she had not been permitted to touch her children for 12 years. She had not shared a meal with another person for 12 years. In fact, because she was considered unclean, it is likely she lived isolated and separated from everyone around her. She would have been considered to be a social outcast because she was unclean — untouched, unloved, and physically sick.

She Suffered at the Hands of Many Physicians

Again, Mark 5:25 and 26 says, "And a certain woman, which had an issue of blood twelve years, And had *suffered many things of* many physicians, and had spent all that she had, and was nothing bettered, but rather grew worse." The word "suffered" is the Greek word *pathos*, which includes both physical and mental suffering. This woman also suffered emotionally.

Mark also states this woman had suffered "*many things*." The Greek word for "many" is *pollous* and describes something huge. This woman had suffered greatly in many, many ways. It is likely that she had anemia because of the loss of blood, which also means she would have been physically very weak. The word "of" is the Greek word *hupo*, meaning *under*. Despite the fact that this woman had been under the care, instruction, influence, and guidance of many physicians for many years, none of them had cured her from this debilitating illness.

The gospel of Luke tells of the same incident. But Luke's perspective as a physician was probably slightly different than Mark's. He recorded in Luke 8:43, "And a woman having an issue of blood twelve years, which had spent all her living upon physicians, neither could be healed of any." Luke records that doctors had tried everything to help this woman but were unable to stop the flow of blood from her body. And the treatments that were used in the First Century to treat women with her condition were horrific.

Again, Mark 5:26 states she "…had suffered many things of many physicians, and had spent all that she had…." The original Greek says she was "depleted of all of her resources." This woman had spent everything.

Sickness is a thief. It steals your time, your relationships, your money, your attention, your mind — it depletes you of *everything*. After this woman had spent everything, verse 26 says, "…she was nothing better, but grew worse." Her finances were completely depleted and yet she was still sick and labeled "unclean."

Faith Arises

Mark 5:27 continues, "When she had *heard* of Jesus, came in the press behind, and touched his garment." In the original Greek, this verse reads, "When she *heard the things concerning Jesus*…." But *how did this woman hear of Jesus?* She had been isolated from other people because of her unclean status according to Levitical Law.

On this particular day, the city was vacant because everyone in the city had gone down to the seashore to meet Jesus as He arrived from the other side. When the woman stepped outside, the streets were vacant and she was able to walk down the roads without people yelling, "Unclean! Unclean!" She could walk freely without being shunned.

We can only imagine that as she wandered through the streets, she wondered what was happening in the city. And as the people began to return and the streets began to be crowded with people again, this *unclean* woman would have tried to hide herself. She understood if she accidentally came in contact with other people and made them unclean, the crowd would have the right to stone her according to the Levitical Law.

As people were passing by, she began to hear about Jesus and how people were being healed. She heard about someone named Jesus who was healing the blind, healing the deaf, healing the lame. And she probably began to think, *Maybe this Jesus can heal me too!* Romans 10:17 says, "So then faith cometh by hearing, and hearing by the word of God." As this woman heard the accounts of others who had been healed by Jesus, faith began to rise in her heart."

Mark 5:27 says, "When she had heard of Jesus, came in the press behind, and touched his garment. The original Greek says, "She touched Him on the bottom of His clothes." This woman was on her hands and knees. She knew she couldn't walk through the crowd because she would make everyone unclean around her. So on her hands and knees, she crawled through the legs of people as they walked by. The Bible says people were thronging Jesus — everyone pushing and straining to get to Him — so they were not even aware that she was in their midst. This woman had faith in her heart and was determined to touch Jesus.

Made Whole

Verse 28 continues, "For she said, If I may touch but his clothes, I shall be whole." The Greek actually says, "For she kept on saying and kept on saying...." This woman was talking to herself as she was coming up behind Jesus, and she kept saying, "If I may but touch His clothes, I shall be *whole*."

The word "whole" is the Greek word *sodzo*, the same Greek word that is also translated "healed" in verse 23. It means *a touch of salvation that brings delivering and healing power that results in wholeness*. It is the New Testament word for *salvation*. She was saying, "*If I can just have a saving touch, I know I will be saved*." When salvation comes, it not only brings spiritual salvation, but it also brings freedom — and it brings relief, and it brings healing!

"And straightway the fountain of her blood was dried up; and she felt in her body that she was healed of that plague" (Mark 5:29). This woman, who had suffered for 12 years and had lost everything she owned going from doctor to doctor trying to find a cure, knew immediately she was healed because the bleeding suddenly stopped!

The Bible tells us Jesus knew immediately that healing power had flowed from Him, and He turned to find who had touched Him. Verse 34 says, "And He said unto her, Daughter, thy faith hath made thee whole; go in *peace*, and be whole of thy plague." The Greek word translated as "peace" is *eirene*, which always denotes *the cessation of war* or *the end of conflict*. It pictures *order in the place of chaos*. *Eirene* literally means, "*Now it is time to begin a period of reconstruction and rebuilding.*" Jesus was telling this woman, "Daughter, now it is time for you to begin rebuilding your life."

Jesus' power healed her. It brought her freedom and saved her. Jesus' power healed her when she reached out by faith and took hold of Him. And *you* can do the same. Take hold of the healing power of God at this very moment. It still works. *Jesus is the same yesterday, today, and forever!* What He did then, He is still doing today! Reach out and receive!

STUDY QUESTIONS

Study to shew thyself approved unto God, a workman that needeth not to be ashamed, rightly dividing the word of truth.
— 2 Timothy 2:15

1. In your own words, describe the scene of Jesus arriving back at the seashore after healing the two men who had been possessed by demons. How did the people respond to Jesus' arrival and why did they respond as they did?
2. What happened as Jairus arrived on the scene? Describe who Jairus was and why he caused such a stir in the throng that surrounded Jesus.
3. Explain why the woman with the issue of blood was isolated from the rest of the people. Describe how she likely heard of Jesus and how she received her healing.

PRACTICAL APPLICATION

> But be ye doers of the word, and not hearers only,
> deceiving your own selves.
> — James 1:22

1. God has always used miracles to attract people to Jesus Christ. John 6:2 says, "And a great multitude followed him, because they saw his miracles which he did on them that were diseased." The multitudes followed Jesus because they saw His miracles! How will you make room in your life to allow Jesus to perform His miracle-working, life-changing power through you?

2. The *RIV (Renner Interpretive Version)* of John 6:2 reads:

    A massive multitude continually followed Jesus because they were constantly seeing the mighty signs He was performing on those who were sick. Those whose health was so deteriorated that they were physically frail were recipients of these mighty deeds that authenticated the fact that God was with Jesus!

Jesus is still the best thing that has ever happened to any person who comes in contact with Him! If you have need of healing or a manifestation of miraculous power, go ahead and believe for a miracle to start working in your life! Just think of the profound effect a single miracle will have on your life personally — and in the lives of the people you know.

Notes

Notes

www.ingramcontent.com/pod-product-compliance
Lightning Source LLC
Chambersburg PA
CBHW060043040426
42331CB00032B/2248